110
Swear Word

Sugar Skulls Coloring Book for Adults

J.C. Charla © 2020

All rights reserved. No part of this book may be reproduced or transmitted in any form or by any means, including but not limited to information storage and retrieval systems, electronic, mechanical, photocopy, recording, etc. without written permission from the copyright holder.

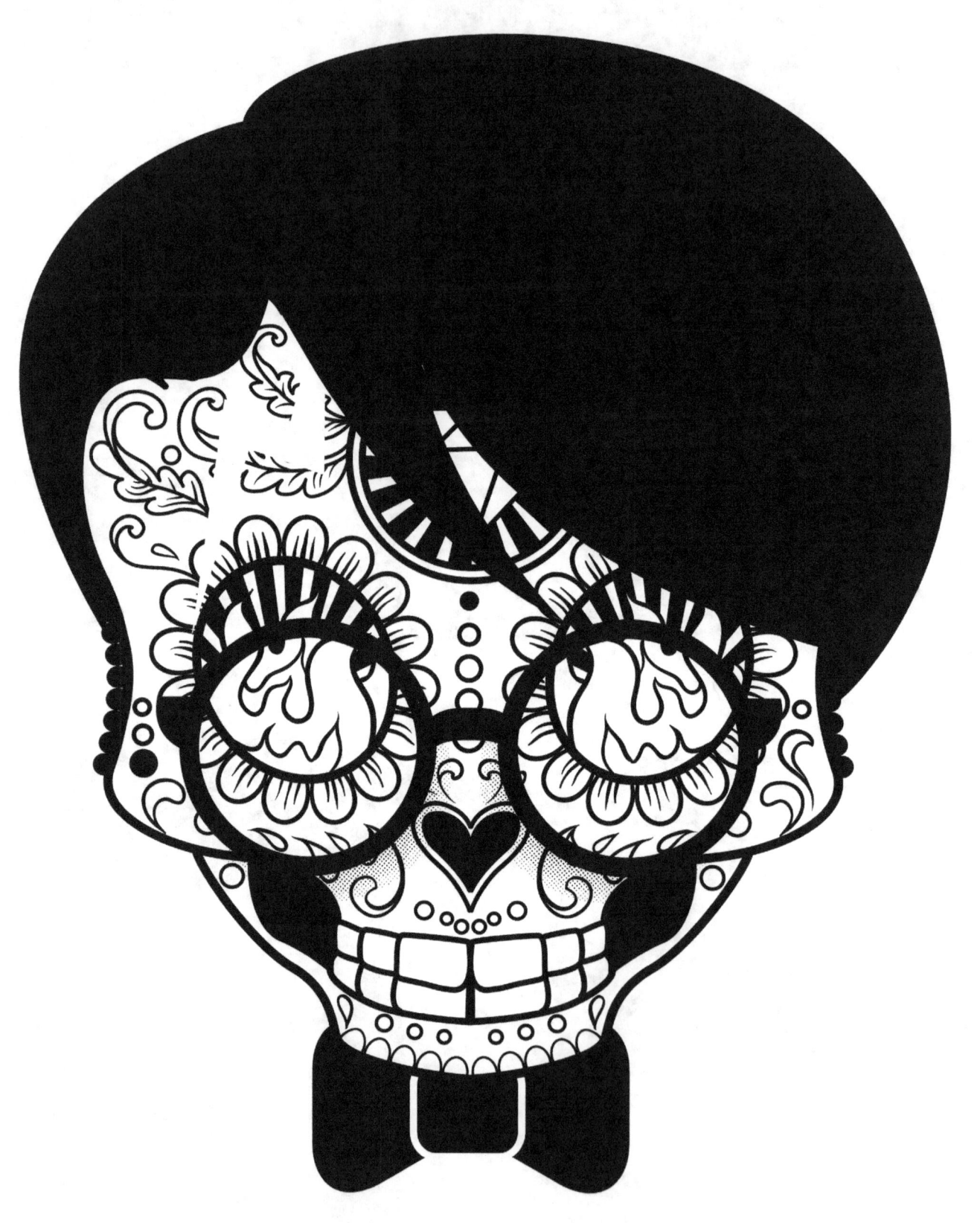

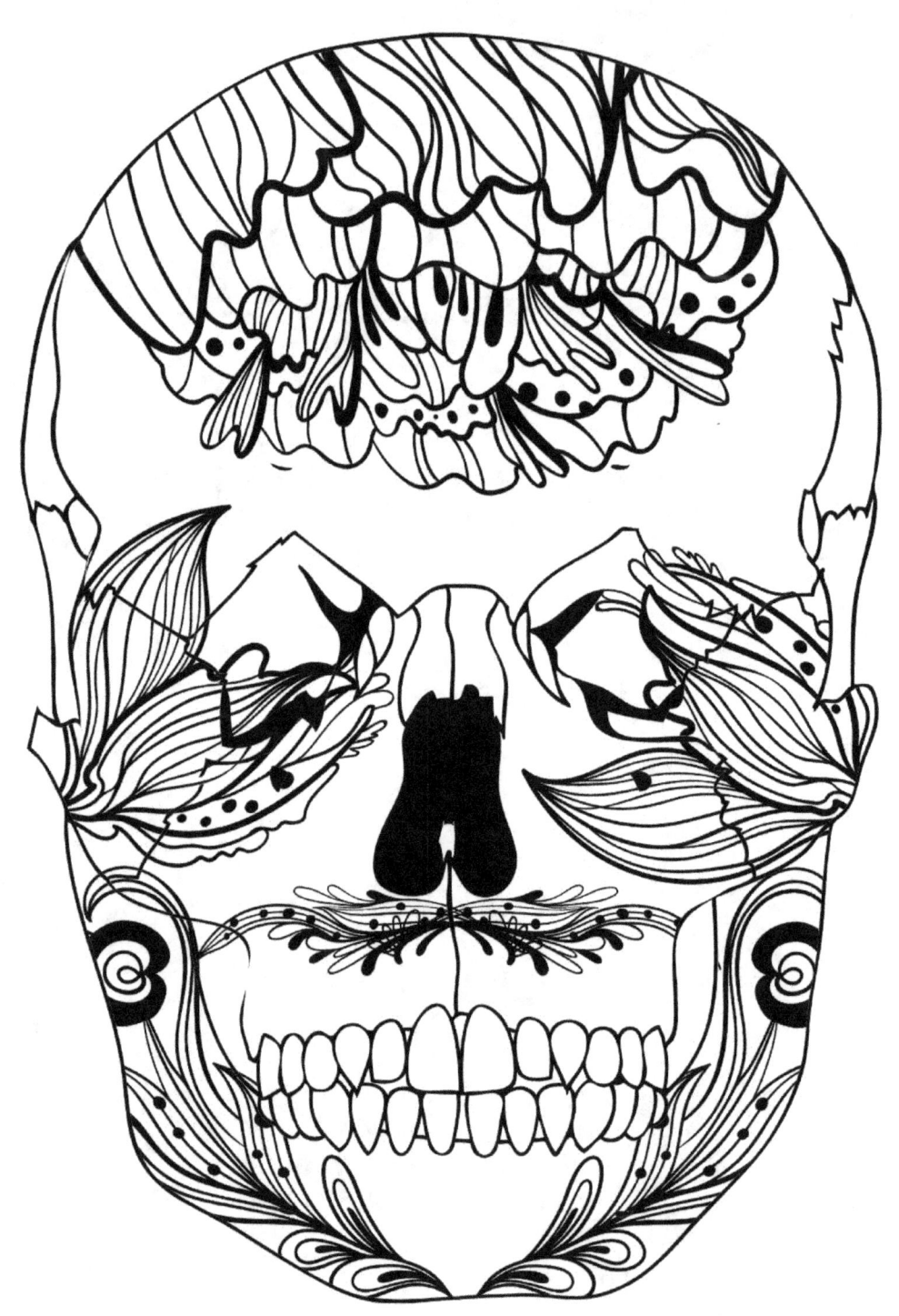

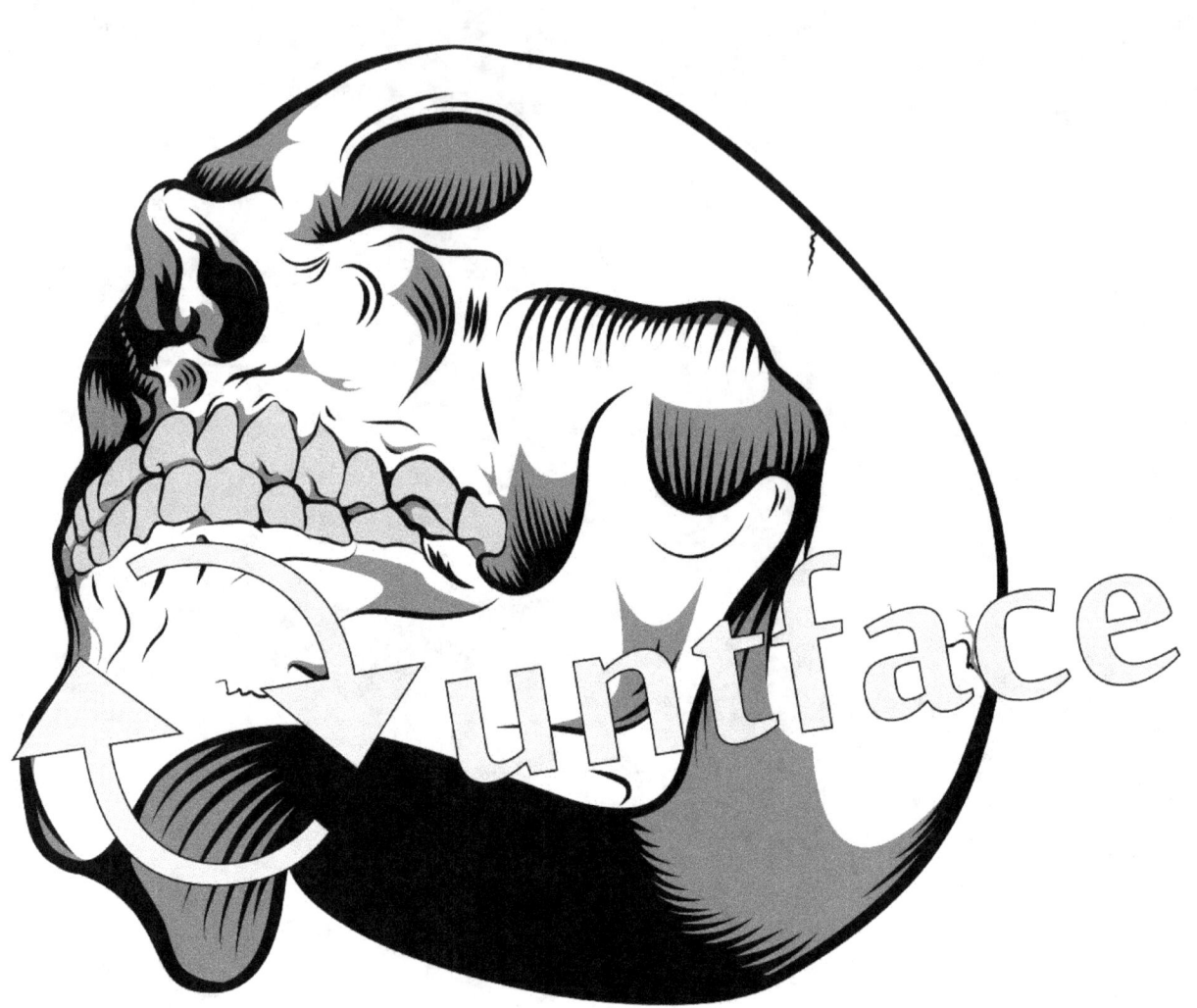

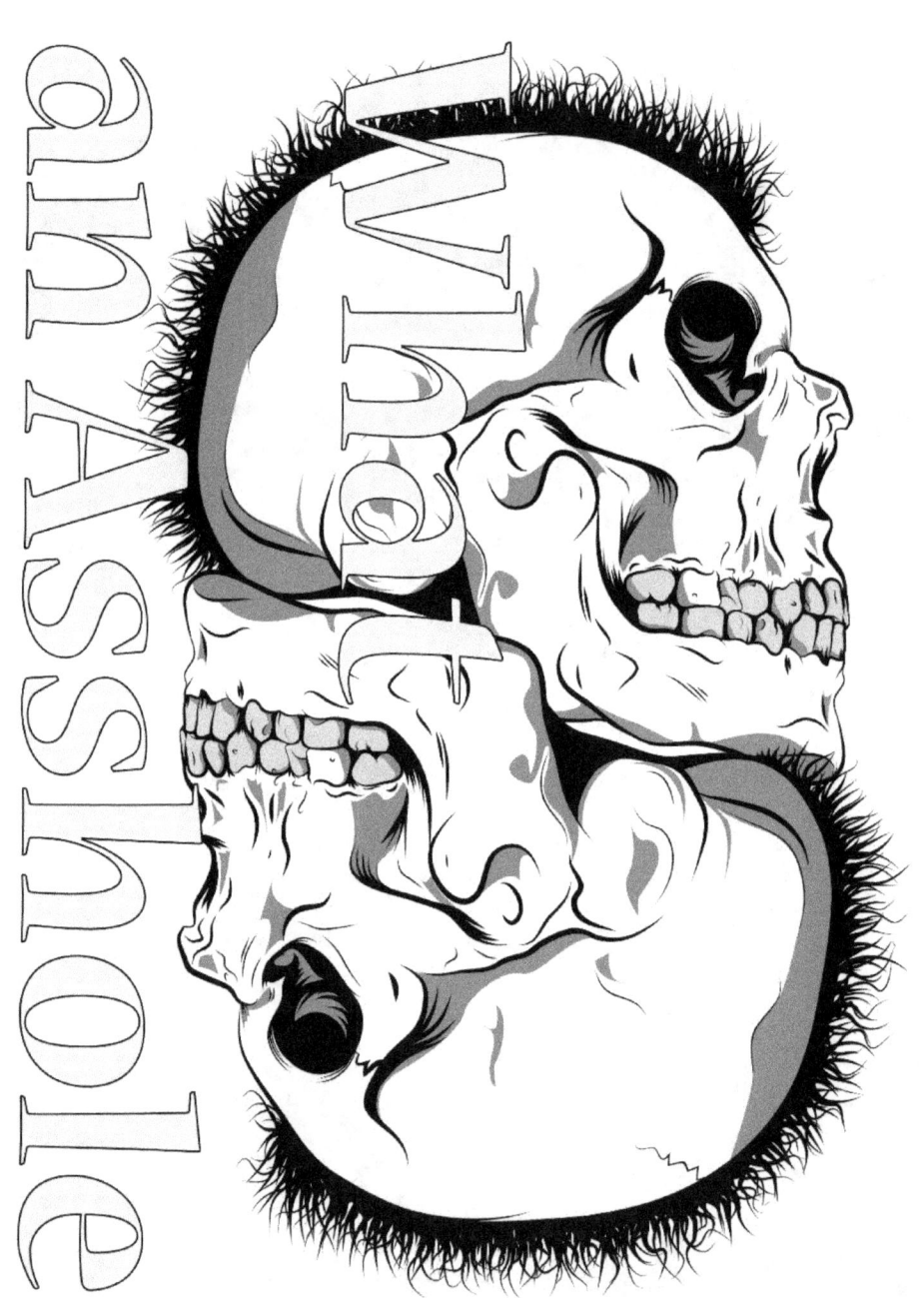

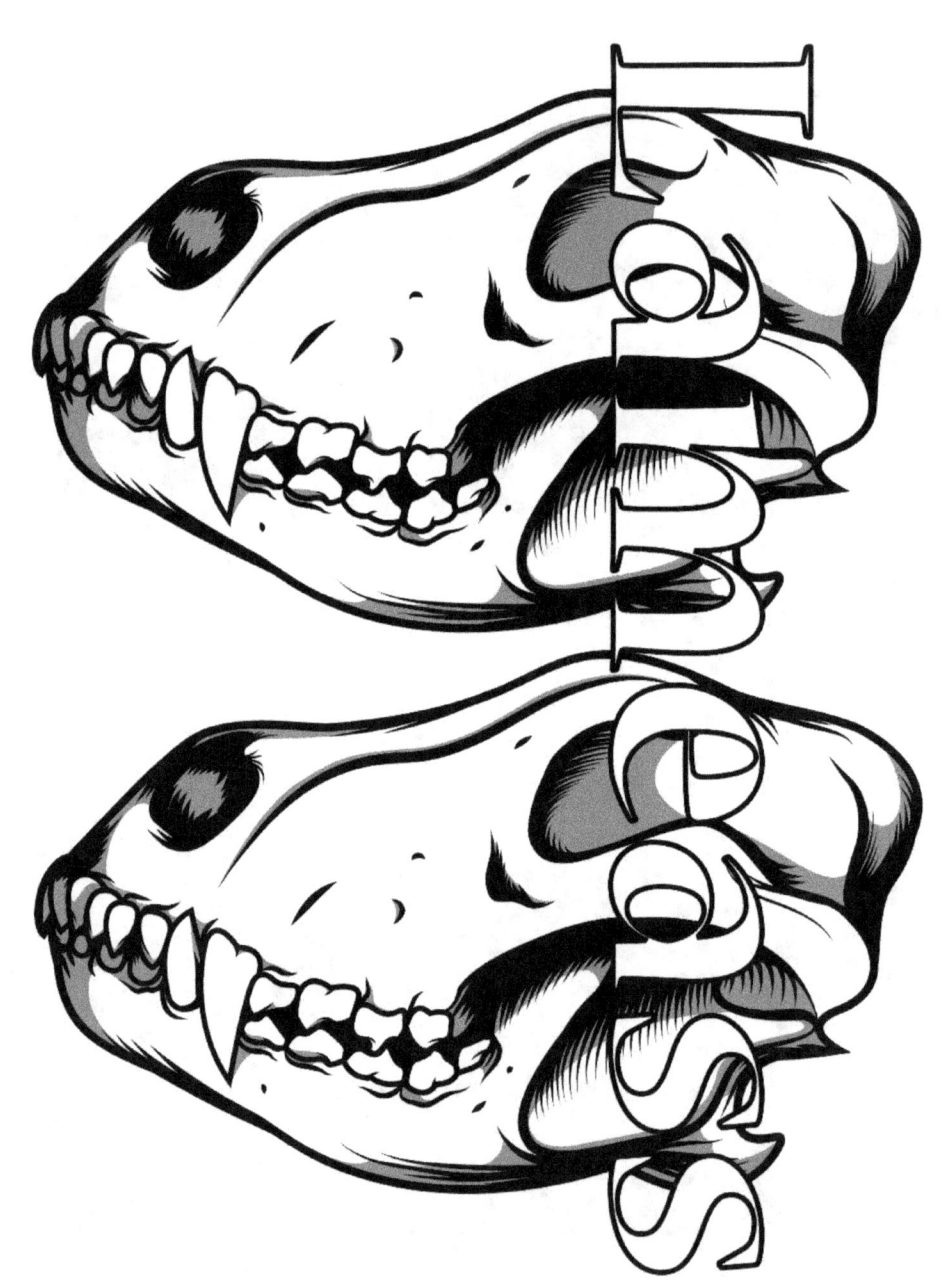

Damn

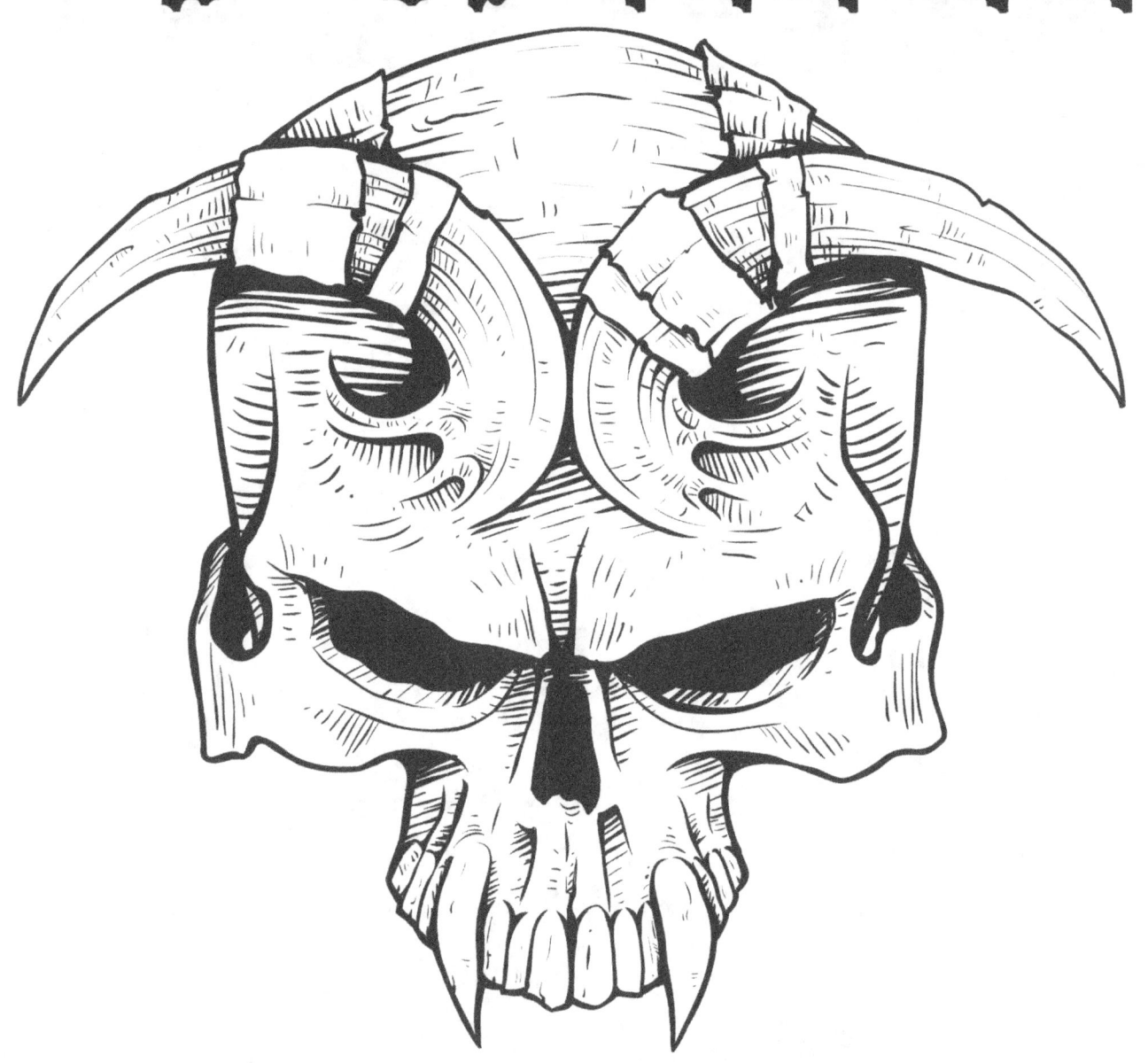

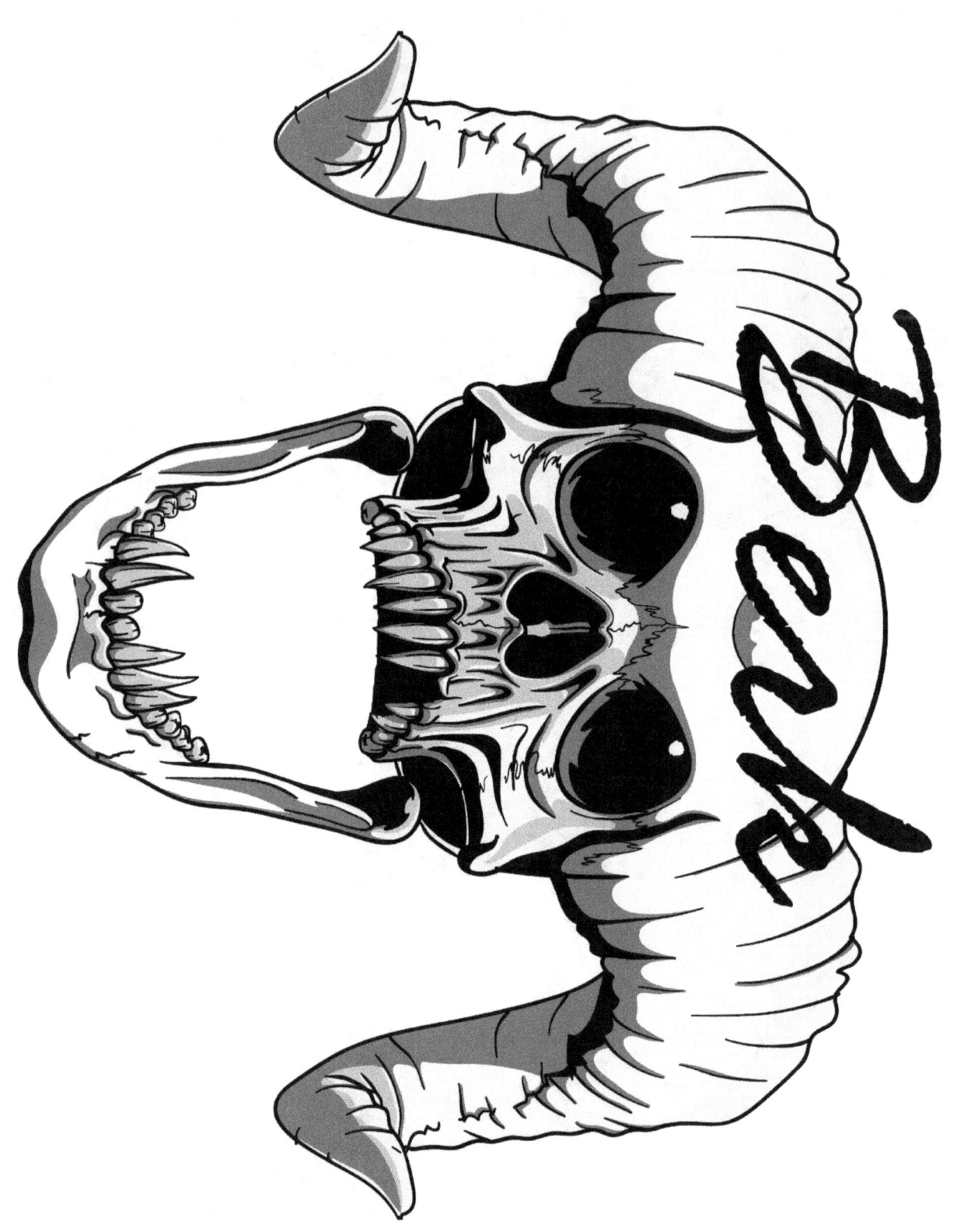

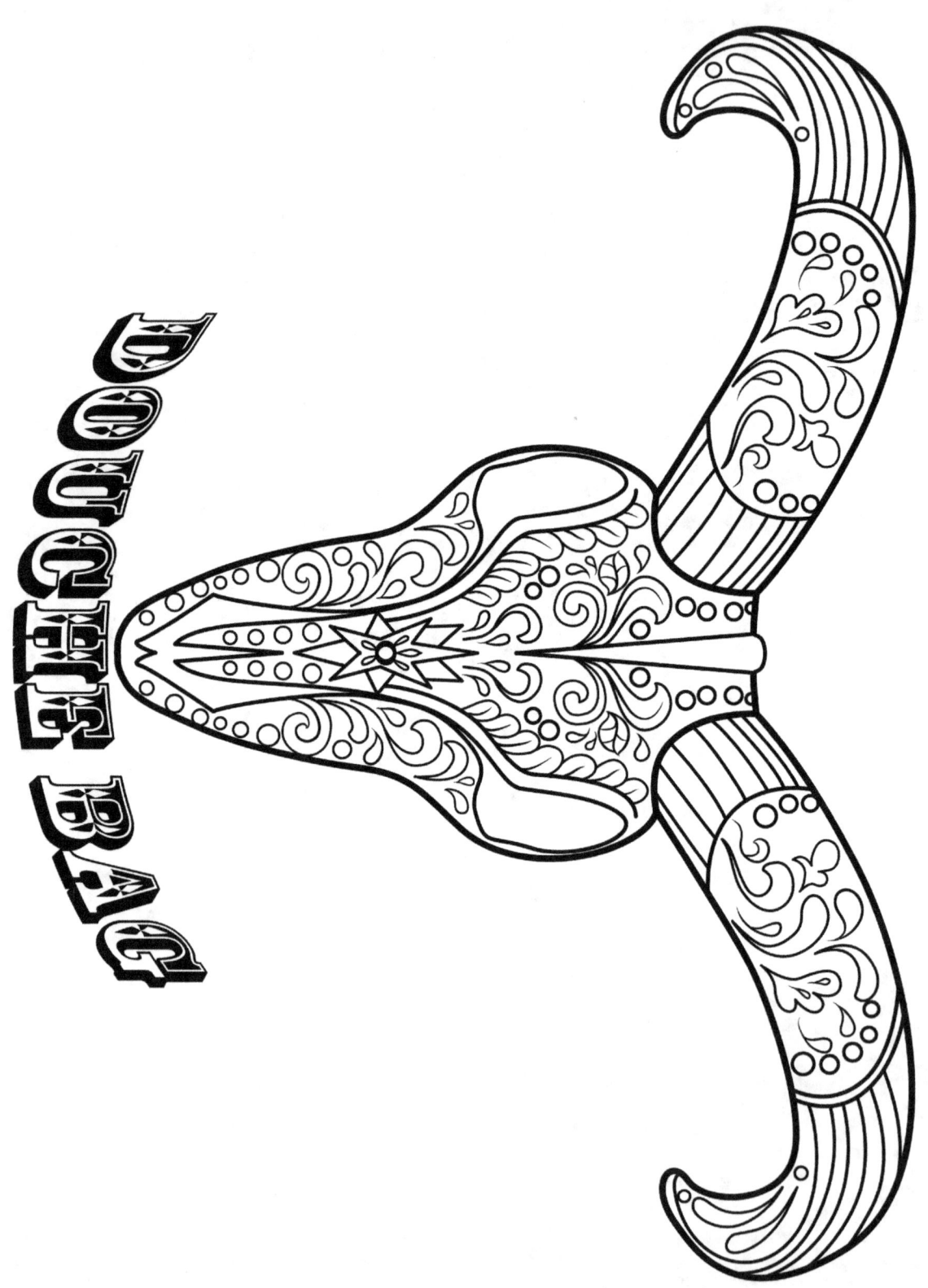